Career Quest

EXPLORING BUILDING TRADE CAREERS

GREG ROBISON

TWENTY-FIRST CENTURY BOOKS / MINNEAPOLIS

Twenty-First Century Books™
An imprint of Lerner Publishing Group, Inc.
241 First Avenue North
Minneapolis, MN 55401 USA

For reading levels and more information, look up this title at www.lernerbooks.com.

Main body text set in Bembo Std Regular.
Typeface provided by Monotype Typography.

Library of Congress Cataloging-in-Publication Data

Names: Robison, Greg, author.
Title: Exploring building trade careers / Greg Robison.
Description: Minneapolis : Twenty-First Century Books, [2026] | Series: Career quest | Includes bibliographical references and index. | Audience: Ages 11–18 | Audience: Grades 7–9 | Summary: "The building trades feature jobs in construction and related fields. Carpenters, plumbers, welders, and more all combine hands-on work with technical skills in these jobs. Find out more about these careers, the education they require, and more"—Provided by publisher.
Identifiers: LCCN 2024037456 (print) | LCCN 2024037457 (ebook) | ISBN 9798765644164 (lib. bdg.) | ISBN 9798765684863 (pbk.) | ISBN 9798765682692 (epub)
Subjects: LCSH: Building trades—Vocational guidance—Juvenile literature.
Classification: LCC TH159 .R63 2026 (print) | LCC TH159 (ebook) | DDC 690.023—dc23/eng/20241228

LC record available at https://lccn.loc.gov/2024037456
LC ebook record available at https://lccn.loc.gov/2024037457

Manufactured in the United States of America
2-1014437-52442-5/4/2026

CONTENTS

INTRODUCTION

When it's time for you to choose a career, it's important to select an occupation that you will enjoy doing. After all, the average person spends forty hours a week, or ninety thousand hours in a lifetime, at work. That's nearly forty-five years! So why not love what you do? If a job that will constantly challenge you, provide hands-on opportunities, and is outside of a traditional office environment sounds interesting, then you should consider a career in building trades.

Building trades professionals specialize in construction and other related fields. These careers usually require a combination of both technical and hands-on skills. Job duties can include building and repairing structures, as well as installing and maintaining different systems. The building trades industry offers a wide range of career opportunities. Professionals are often paid well, have options to advance their career, and make a difference in the communities they live and work in. Some, but not all, of the possible trades include:

Learning more about your interests and strengths is the first step to choosing a career.

Carpenters. Carpenters work on many different types of projects, including commercial buildings, residential homes, furniture, and creative decorative items. Carpenters also complete a variety of tasks, including reading blueprints and designs, choosing appropriate building materials, and using a wide array of tools to help build projects.

Electricians. Electricians not only help keep everyone's lights on, but also connect entire cities, help ensure that households can run smoothly, maintain phone and internet lines, and even run solar and wind energy turbines. Plus, the building trades industry needs more electricians; the electrical industry is slated to grow more than 6 percent by 2031.

HVAC technicians. HVAC stands for heating, ventilation, and air-conditioning. HVAC technicians help homes and businesses stay cool in the summer and warm in the winter. They install and maintain heating and air systems, making sure that they are working properly and providing both comfort and air quality.

Plumbers. Plumbers install and repair water and gas pipes. They work on a variety of different jobsites and sometimes even introduce new technologies to their clients such as digital leak detectors, tankless water heaters, and various smart appliances. And, since they deal with water, steam, gas, and other elements, plumbers help make sure that all a building's mechanical systems are operating properly.

Welders. Welders play a major role in both construction and design. Being a welder allows someone to show off skills such as creative thinking and meticulous precision work. Be prepared to stay busy in a career as a welder. Their responsibilities include accurately marking weld points, assuring that they have accurate weld alignments, and applying the right finishes to improve both the strength and design of the fabricated structures.

This book covers what it takes to enter these building trades and more, reasons to consider a career in this industry, and some of the challenges that you might face. It will also explore some of the most popular jobs in the industry and help you select the one that is best for you.

CHAPTER ONE

Laying the Foundation

Do you like a challenge? Do you enjoy working with your hands and creating new things? Would you rather work somewhere other than a traditional office? If you answered yes to any of those questions, then a career in building trades might be right for you.

Building trades refer to the trades and professions concerned with the planning, creation, and finishing of structures. Experts work every step of the way to build the best, safest, and most affordable homes and businesses. From electricians who wire lights to plumbers who ensure there is running water, the need for building trades never ends. These trades are essential to and chiefly practiced in connection with building construction. But what are the benefits of working in building trades? Jennifer Goodman, the executive director of the New Hampshire Preservation Alliance, listed a few: "High job satisfaction, positive trends like the trades becoming more welcoming to women, and strong examples of . . . mentorships and training." Let's explore a few more.

Get a Jump on Your Career

Many careers in the building trades follow an apprentice model, which means that when you decide to pursue an opportunity in this industry, you can often begin working with on-the-job training through an apprenticeship program. Chapter three covers apprenticeships more, but here are some of the benefits of them:

- Complete industry credentials and certifications while still earning a paycheck
- Avoid large student loans
- Start earning money right away

High Demand

Building trades are important for the construction, maintenance, and repair of buildings, infrastructure, and transportation equipment. Skilled workers are always in high demand in these fields, especially as the population and economy continue to grow. Additionally, many older workers are retiring from their jobs. By the mid-2020s, more than 40 percent of trade workers were over the age of forty-five. As these older workers retire, their positions will need to be filled quickly.

Competitive Pay

The building trades industry can offer competitive pay in return for your hard work. In fact, many people earn high five-figure, and even six-figure, salaries. And you don't necessarily need to obtain a college degree to earn these high salaries. Plus, because of the high demand for building trades professionals, many companies are willing to spend more money on their employees to get the skills needed to complete important job projects.

Worker Benefits

In addition to often earning a high salary in the building trades industry, workers also usually receive benefits. These can include health and dental insurance, paid time off, sick leave, unemployment insurance, and much more.

Job Satisfaction

Building trades professionals report higher job satisfaction than those in other professions. More than 80 percent say they would choose the same career again. It also often feels good knowing that you help provide real-world solutions to challenges, and you can see the results of your hard work everywhere you look. Look around your community; people who chose a career in building trades contributed to all the buildings, schools, roads, restaurants, stores, and homes.

Advancement Opportunities

Building trades can provide many opportunities for job growth and development. While on the job, you can develop your skills, learn new ones, and open the door for future promotions. Many building trades careers also offer certification opportunities. These are chances to learn more

Continuing education can lead to job opportunities, increased pay, and a bigger network of industry professionals.

skills and receive official credit or training licenses, which can help advance your career and increase your income. Many people in the industry have risen through the ranks, starting as apprentices or entry-level workers, adding years of experience to their trade, and obtaining new roles.

Work-Life Balance

Unlike many professionals who take their work home with them most nights, when you work in the building trades, you always complete your tasks on the jobsite. That means when you leave work, you can focus on the things you want to, including family, friends, hobbies, and other activities. Having a strong work-life balance—that is, being able to devote enough time and energy to both your job and your personal life—also contributes to your mental health and happiness, along with greater job satisfaction. Workers who have a good work-life balance are 12 percent more productive at work. And more than 70 percent of all employees say they take work-life balance into account when choosing a job.

Creative, Engaging Work

Chances are that you will never be bored with a career in building trades. Unlike many offices, no two jobsites are ever the same. And each day will provide different challenges and opportunities. The industry is also constantly evolving, which means you'll have the chance to experiment with different techniques and check out new materials, tools, and technologies. There's always a lot to learn and to be excited about.

Job Security

Employees with job security know they are unlikely to be fired, laid off, or otherwise dismissed. And even if a job ends, it is not as difficult to find a new one in building trades. There will always be a need for skilled workers in the building trades since they work on the infrastructure that is critical for societies to function, such as electricity, plumbing, roads, and bridges. You can be assured that you are in a stable industry with many opportunities.

The High-Tech Future of the Building Trades

The building trades industry is in the middle of a technological shift. Workers are beginning to trade their old-school paper processes for digital apps, and there are even drones buzzing around some jobsites.

While traditional project sites are associated with big machines, loud noise, and sometimes costly delays, many companies are learning how beneficial going high tech can be. Designing, building, and operating job projects using a 3D model and digital construction before the project ever takes shape in the physical world allows companies to cut waste, employee time, and building materials. Additionally, team builders work together more effectively by connecting through mobile devices and using both virtual and augmented reality to make project decisions. Plus, project teams can use data gathered from past projects by machine learning technology. This data helps them make more informed decisions, manage risks, budget time, and improve worker safety on jobsites.

It is an exciting time to join the building trades industry. If you are interested in joining the workforce, you may be one of the first to see commercial applications of drones, robotics, and laser scanners being used on a jobsite.

Flexible Career Options

There are so many different careers to choose from in the building trades industry. Whether you are creative, mathematically inclined, a born problem-solver, or a natural leader, chances are there's something that you will be interested in. Plus, the industry is constantly changing and evolving. Because there are so many opportunities, the path you start out on in the building trades might not be the one you stay with. But a solid foundation in building skills will translate well to other jobs in the industry if you decide to try something new.

Freedom to Travel

Want to see the world and get paid for it, rather than working at the same place every day? Since there is such an incredibly high demand for building trades professionals all over the country, there is no limit to where your career can take you. Whether you decide to move around on your own by working with different companies or choose to pursue a job with a national or global company, the travel opportunities are endless. The building trades industry is growing in every country, state, and city around the world.

CHAPTER TWO

First Steps

A job in the building trades can be very challenging yet rewarding. And it's never too early to start preparing for your future. Here are some ways to get a jump start on the road to success in the building trades.

Stay Focused on Graduating

In addition to being at least eighteen years of age, most building trade opportunities require that you have a high school diploma or graduate equivalency degree/general education diploma (GED). Above all else, you should focus on earning your degree to prepare for a job in the building trades. "Graduating from high school is not just something to check off to move to higher levels of education," Luke Greiner, an employment researcher, said. "Students are gaining highly sought-after employment skills [in school]." Knowing how to communicate, solve problems, pay attention to detail, and basic technology skills are all things that can be learned in high school, no matter what your future.

Many jobs require a high school diploma or equivalent just to apply.

Take Relevant Courses and Hone Your Skills

While it's great to have hands-on knowledge of a skill or craft, most of the building trades want their potential employees and apprentices to possess strong theoretical knowledge as well. That knowledge can come from classes. Some recommended topics that you might want to focus on if you're interested in the building trades include construction, math, science, and woodshop courses.

Some other great skills to have include blueprint reading and mechanical skills. Some things can be learned on the job. But knowing everything you can beforehand will set you apart as a job candidate. Anywhere you can get extra experience—whether it's signing up for a more difficult class, finding a mentor on the weekend to tutor you, or tackling an extra-credit project—is a benefit. Plus, learning to read plans, follow directions, ask questions, problem-solve, and communicate well are all essential traits for a successful career in the industry.

Obtain Your Driver's License

There are some building trades jobs where you won't need a driver's license. People who work on crews that get rides to jobs may not need one. However, many certifications require one. Some equipment may require a driver's license too—if not also a commercial license to operate heavy machinery. And some employers see a driver's license as proof of their employee's general reliability.

Start Gaining Experience

While it's true that most careers or training programs in building trades require employees to be at least eighteen years of age, there are many job opportunities available for you to check out before then that will help you develop a skill set that will support your future career in building trades. These opportunities will

Having a driver's license and reliable transportation is one step toward success at finding and keeping a job.

help you learn more about various tools and equipment, working with your hands, and how to interact with your fellow team members. Here are some examples:

- Hardware store employees learn how to work with both customers and coworkers. They also get up close and personal looks at various tools and equipment.
- Landscaping and nursery employees work outdoors and use their bodies every day. Some trade jobs require physical labor, such as lifting heavy items.

- Summer camp counselors are responsible for younger campers, work with their peers, and take direction from camp directors.
- Farm laborers do a little bit of everything, from working with other people to taking care of animals to fixing machines that break down.
- Sports team assistants at local schools learn teamwork, strategy, and how to support others. They may work with just one part of the team, but their work benefits the whole team.

Every experience that gives you a combination of leadership and teamwork is valuable.

- Tech or prop crew members build and design sets, learn how to cue and operate sounds and lights, and communicate with actors and directors for a seamless performance.

Don't forget the most important part of your summer or part-time gig: always show up on time and ready to work, have a positive attitude and work hard, and obtain a good reference from your employer when you're done. This will help build your reputation as someone that your next employers can count on. Many jobs ask for references too, so having someone who will speak highly of you is both an ego boost and a benefit for future work.

Do Your Research

There are a lot of jobs available in the building trades industry. In fact, there are more than thirty building trades to choose from! While variety can be a good thing, it's important to explore all the trades that you are interested in to help find the best fit. Try to choose something that you will enjoy doing. Take the time to do your research. Check out career opportunities online and read books that will help you learn more about them. Talk to your school guidance counselor or a friend or family member who has experience in the industry. There's always more to know.

Consider a Mentorship

It's always a good idea to ask for advice and support when you need it. Having a mentor can be a great way to help prepare for a career in the building trades. A mentor can help you build relationships with building trades companies, trade schools, and employment partners. Additionally, they can help answer questions and provide useful resources for research, training, and employment opportunities that will assist you as you begin your career. You can find out more about mentorship programs by talking with your school guidance counselor, visiting building trade industry websites online, and checking what mentoring programs are available in your state or region.

Internship Programs

Many building trades companies offer internship programs that allow you to learn more about a career in the industry. Interns gain valuable hands-on experience, and some even get paid. The main goal of an internship program is to prepare future workers for their chosen career. They also allow young people to meet and network with people already in the industry.

Some ways to find an internship program include identifying a trade in which you want to complete an internship, reaching out to any personal connections, and checking out online resources and internship postings. And be sure to bring your A game when preparing for an internship interview. Internship placements can be very competitive, so being prepared, professional, and confident can show a company why you are the best candidate.

Job Shadowing

Job shadowing allows people interested in a trade to accompany another employee while on the job. It is a time

Shadow someone you trust. A good job shadowing experience can be encouraging and educational.

to watch and learn and ask any questions you may have. You may only have an afternoon, or you may have several weeks. You will get to see what is expected of employees, what the workplace is like, and get a feel for the industry as a whole. Ask around for job shadowing opportunities or ask any professionals you know. During a job shadow, take notes, follow the workplace rules, come with a positive attitude, and try to get the most out of your time in the field.

Setting Yourself Apart

Looking for some additional ways to help prepare you for a career in the building trades? Check out some of the following ideas that will get you started on your path to success.

Focus on Improving Your Soft Skills

Soft skills are attributes and non-technical skills that help you interact, manage your work, and solve problems on the job. Working in building trades can be technical and hands-on; however, communication, attention to detail, dependability, and working well with a team are important skills to concentrate on as well. Take the time to focus on these areas—it will help show employers that you are well-rounded and will help you with your future work.

Volunteer to Work in the Trades

Don't become discouraged if you are not offered an internship right away. Another great way to gain job experience is to volunteer for a company in the building trades. If you have the time, offer to work as a helper on a construction site or in a company shop. This would help you learn more about what you would be doing on a day-to-day basis, as well as learn skills and techniques from managers and employees that have been working in the industry for a long time. And who knows? It just might result in a job offer down the road.

Answering assessment test questions can be hard. Talking about desires and dreams might seem scary. But you are the only one who knows the real you.

Take an Aptitude Test

Taking a career aptitude test is a great way to help determine career choices that you might want to consider. Some common tests that are available include the Myers-Briggs Type Indicator, the Holland Code Career Aptitude Test, and the Princeton Review Career Quiz. If you are really interested in learning about obtaining a career in the building trades, you should consider taking the Construction and Skilled Trades exam. This test will help provide potential employers with a measure of your skills, aptitude, knowledge, and ability to perform your desired job. Study guides and online test prep courses are available, so check with your school guidance counselor or online to get further information. Some exams or study guides are free. Others have fees attached. Sometimes employers will cover the fee for you.

CHAPTER THREE

Path Ahead

Many building trades careers encourage or even require apprenticeships to begin your career. Apprenticeship is a practice that dates back thousands of years. It's a time-tested training method that combines on-the-job training experiences with job-related technical education. Companies around the world in the building trades industry have benefited from utilizing apprenticeships to help job trainees learn more about their new career and what it takes to become successful. During your training as an apprentice, you gain knowledge and skills that are specific to your industry and earn money while learning your trade. Plus, apprenticeships allow you to gain skill sets that will help you advance your career later and prepare you for new opportunities in your industry. Since program requirements can vary by state and province, be sure to check out your local license boards through state or federal departments of labor for further information.

Apprenticeships can benefit employees and employers, allowing both sides to find the perfect fit.

Reasons to Consider an Apprenticeship

When you decide to pursue a career in the building trades industry, there are many reasons to consider entering an apprenticeship program. "If one fully embraces the role of an apprentice early in their career," said founder of leadership company Skybound Coaching and Training, Glenn Taylor, "it can foster a lifelong sense of curiosity, openness, and humility—all crucial qualities in the most successful leaders." Let's check out some of the other benefits.

Gain Hands-On Experience

One of the great things about an apprenticeship is that you get to spend your time on the job gaining hands-on experience, as well as learning about new skills in a classroom setting. It gives you the chance to merge theory and book learning with practical knowledge. This way, you can expect to spend time learning and practicing job-specific skills that you will be using daily in your future career.

Earn a Paycheck Faster

When you begin your career through an apprenticeship program, you earn as you learn. This makes it easier to support yourself financially and pay for necessities such as rent as you establish a career. And since apprenticeships are paid, you don't gain student loan debt during them, which can be difficult to pay off later.

Build Your Network

Apprentices can learn and work with seasoned professionals who have been in their respective fields for a long time. In addition to learning a lot from a variety of different people, this helps you begin establishing a network of colleagues that you can connect with, learn from, and work with throughout your career. This network can help provide referrals to companies and employers. Knowing a variety of people already in the industry can also help you see or decide what your future might include. Do you want to be a business owner or work on a certain type of project? Being able to draw on other peoples' years of experience is a benefit of networking.

Different Types of Apprenticeship Programs in Building Trades

There are several different apprenticeship programs in the building trades industry. Each one has unique benefits. Here are three popular options:

Electrician

Electricity doesn't require years of schooling since you can join an apprenticeship instead. The pay range for an apprenticeship varies based on your location, but it typically averages from $29 to $32 per hour. The average length of an apprenticeship is four years and includes eight thousand hours of hands-on and classroom learning. Gaining enough experience to replace retiring workers takes effort since companies are often looking for workers with abundant experience who can take over existing workloads. "You need a very long lead time in order to ramp up [working] capacity," Josh Hawley, the director of the Ohio Education Research Center, said. But once earned, the jobs are there.

HVAC Technician

Like an electrician program, an apprenticeship program in the HVAC industry consists of both classroom and on-the-job training and generally lasts about four years, with more than eight thousand hours of training. Pay ranges can vary based on where you work, but you can expect to earn a wage averaging $30 an hour. With the number of HVAC units worldwide expected to reach 5.6 billion by 2050, the need for technicians is growing too.

Plumber

Deciding on a career in the plumbing trade can mean a stable job that benefits the whole community. Wherever clean water is necessary, so are plumbers. The average pay range for a plumbing apprenticeship is between $17 and $27 per hour. Plumbing apprenticeship programs generally last approximately four years and include up to nine thousand hours total of on-the-job and classroom training experience.

How to Get an Apprenticeship in the Building Trades

If you decide you want to do an apprenticeship, you might be wondering how to get started. The following steps explain how to begin securing an apprenticeship in the building trades.

Pick a Trade

There are many exciting career options available in the building trades industry. Make sure to research the trades that interest you the most and will match your personality and skill set. Some jobs share similarities—for example, HVAC technicians and electricians need to know a lot of the same skills. Builders and plumbers both need to know about construction and layout. But there are differences across the board too. Some jobs require interacting with people, while others need workers who can work independently. Some send workers over a wide area, while others keep them closer to home.

Apprenticeships are investments in yourself and your future.

Finding Possible Apprenticeships

North America's Building Trades Union has 1,900 training centers across the country. They train more than 70 percent of all construction apprentices. The US Department of Labor also has a program that oversees registered apprenticeships. Carpentry, painting, glassworking, and masonry are a few unlicensed trade apprenticeships. Plumbing, pipefitting, and electricians are examples of licensed apprenticeships. And there are specialty trades, including metalwork, insulation, and operating engineers, that can be found through unions.

Start the Application Process

Once you have decided which trade you are most interested in, reach out to the appropriate construction trade unions and training centers in your state or province who can assist you through the application process. Unions help ensure workers receive the assistance and support they need. You can also check out additional resources online for information on apprenticeship programs, as well as tips and tricks to help you and your application stand out.

Be Prepared

You will want to be prepared so that your apprenticeship application shines. First make sure that you meet all the requirements to apply, such as age and level of education. Next, review your application alone or with a trusted adult to make sure you filled out everything correctly.

Follow Up

Don't just sit at home and wait for the phone to ring. Reach out to the company, contractor, or trade union that you have submitted your application to. This lets them know that you would like to be considered for the position. It can help set you apart from other applicants and show the hiring manager that you are genuinely interested in the opportunity.

Interview

If a hiring manager likes the application, then the next step in the application process is an interview. First and foremost, make sure that you are on time for your interview. If the interview is in person or over video, then dress appropriately. Business casual options, such as slacks and a nice shirt, often work well. Research the company that you are applying with and have a list of questions ready to ask the hiring manager, such as what the expected roles and responsibilities, benefits, and advancement opportunities are. Above all, aim to be professional and confident and to explain why you are the best candidate for this opportunity.

Apprenticeship Program Offer

The hiring manager may make you an on-the-spot offer after you have completed your initial interview. Sometimes they will need additional time if they have numerous candidates or ask for a second interview. When you receive an offer for a position in an apprenticeship program, you'll also receive a list of duties and responsibilities, pay rate, projected start date, training schedule, and other information to help prepare you for your new job. But you don't have to accept right

Job
<Application>
Learn the basics and build your own web page!
START
EASY STYLE
DISPLAY PROPERTIES
SCALABLE

<html>
<body>
code*

away. Don't be afraid to ask questions or request extra time to accept the position. There are many things to think about, including the pay, benefits, and commute.

Understand What the Apprenticeship Offers

Although it's often exciting to be selected for an apprenticeship program and you will likely be eager to get started, stop and consider other factors such as your schedule before accepting the offer. For example, how many hours will be spent on the job and how many in school? What knowledge and skills will you need to perform this job? Will your apprenticeship provide the tools you need to perform the job, or will you be expected to provide your own? The more that you know what will be expected, the better prepared you will be to commit to the program.

Apply Now, Even If You Have to Wait

If you have done your research, found an apprenticeship program that you are truly excited about, and understand what it takes to do a great job, then you can apply as soon as you have the opportunity. Sometimes an apprenticeship may not be available immediately, or hiring is limited. Don't let that discourage you. Complete your application so that you will be ready when there are openings. Some places also allow you to submit an application even when there aren't openings, which can let employers know you're interested and make it easier to actually apply when the time comes.

CHAPTER FOUR

Choosing Your Future

One of the great things about a career in the building trades is the number of jobs or trade options that are available. Many building trades jobs also come with salaries near or above the US median household income of $74,580. In some of these jobs, you can even earn six figures once you have gained valuable experience. Check out some of the interesting career paths that are available in the building trades.

Plumber

Every day is a new adventure when you are a plumber. For example, you may help a homeowner or business out if you repair their burst pipe or an overflowing sink. You might be installing, repairing, or maintaining a plumbing system. Sometimes a tankless water heater, low-flush toilet, or a low-flow shower needs to be installed, which helps people save money on their utility bills. You might help educate your clients on greywater recycling. Greywater recycling utilizes used or

Plumbers are needed for everyday jobs and for emergencies. They save water and energy and ensure people can live comfortably.

dirty water collected from certain appliances or drains and is redirected for other purposes, such as watering plants, which helps reduce the environmental impact of water usage.

Plumbers work hard learning and advancing their craft when they are on the job every day. The national average salary of a plumber is $61,550 per year, according to the US Bureau of Labor Statistics. Plus, there's plenty of room to grow in your career and earn even more money.

To begin your career in the plumbing trades, the first thing you will need is to earn your high school diploma or GED certificate. Your next step will be to complete an apprenticeship program. Afterward, you will be able to earn your journeyman license, which states you have completed an apprenticeship and are fully qualified as an electrician. The requirements to obtain this license vary by location, so be sure to research your state's guidelines. Next, you can become a master plumber by earning your master or contractor license. Requirements vary by state. After completing these steps, the sky's the limit. You can advance your plumbing career by becoming a general, service, or sales manager, or even explore starting your own company.

Electrician

A career in the electrical trades can be both challenging and rewarding. You will wear a lot of hats as an electrician. Your job responsibilities can include installing, repairing, and maintaining electrical components, wiring systems, and controls. You will also contribute to more energy-efficient options for homes and businesses by installing solar panels, wind turbines, smart thermostats and appliances, and LED lights. That work puts you on the forefront of cutting-edge technologies that will help protect the environment and save important energy resources.

Your hard work and effort can really pay off. The average salary of an electrician in the United States is $61,590 per year.

The journey to becoming an electrician starts with earning your high school diploma or GED certificate. Next, you will begin your apprenticeship. Once you have completed that, you can then earn a journeyman electrical license, and, after holding that for at least two years, your master or contractor license if you pass a master electrical exam. Requirements for all types of licensures vary depending on where you live. State or federal departments of labor and industry can give further information on completing your licensing and certification programs. When you complete these steps, you can explore advancement opportunities such as becoming a field, general, or sales manager, or maybe owning your own company.

HVAC Technician

It often feels great when your career involves working in a job that positively impacts your community. And that's exactly what HVAC technicians do. When you work in the heating and cooling trade, you help homes and businesses safeguard their indoor air quality, which helps keep people safe from allergens and pollutants. Chances are that you won't ever become bored as an HVAC technician. Some days, you might be installing a more energy-efficient heating or cooling system or replacing one that has become obsolete. Others, you might be working on a cutting-edge new project such as a wind farm or research lab. You might also have the opportunity to install or repair an air conditioner or heater in a car or truck. The bottom line is that wherever you need air-conditioning or heating, you will find an HVAC pro. The average salary of an HVAC technician is $57,300 per year.

If pursuing a career in the HVAC trades sounds good to you, you will first need to graduate from high school or earn your GED certificate. Your next step will be to complete an apprenticeship program or to work on a jobsite under the supervision of a licensed contractor for at least two years. Like other sectors of the building trades, HVAC licensing and certification requirements vary by state, so be sure to check your location for further information. Additionally, the Environmental Protection Agency requires that all HVAC technicians regardless of state complete an exam on the proper handling of refrigerants. Once you have completed the work experience requirements and passed the refrigerant exam, you can apply for your contractor license, which will include also passing the licensing exam for your state or province. After you become a licensed contractor, many HVAC opportunities will open for you, including becoming a warehouse, installation, or service manager, or starting your own HVAC business.

Pipefitter

As a pipefitter, your main responsibilities entail building and maintaining piping systems for a wide range of purposes. Pipefitters install and maintain pipes that carry chemicals, acids, and gases. They sometimes help design, install, and repair pipe systems in power plants, as well as HVAC systems. As a pipefitter, you can also choose from a variety of different industrial fields to work in such as construction or manufacturing because they all rely on low- or high-pressure piping systems. Depending on where you get hired, you can expect to earn an average salary of up to $69,000 per year.

When you are ready to pursue a career as a pipefitter, your first step is to earn your high school diploma or GED

Skilled welders are the heart of infrastructure, from basic household goods to the cars we drive to the buildings in which we live.

equivalent, just like in the other building trades. Most pipefitters learn their trade through a four- or five-year apprenticeship program. Like other apprenticeships that we have previously discussed, apprentices in the pipefitting industry will typically receive paid, on-the-job training in addition to classroom instruction. Classroom training includes job safety, blueprint reading, mathematics, chemistry, and applied physics. While most pipefitter workers enter an apprenticeship directly, some also start out working directly for a business as general helpers who hold materials, fetch tools, and clean work areas.

Welder

Do you enjoy working with tools? Do creative problem-solving, performing detail-oriented projects, and working with math and numbers interest you? If so, you might want to consider welding as a career option. As a welder, you play an important role in the construction and design processes. You have the opportunity to perform many different tasks on the job. You may work on an arc welding project, which uses electrical currents to create heat and bond metals together. Or you may use heat to cut and trim metal objects to specific dimensions. Perhaps you will use your soldering or brazing (which uses heat to join two or more metal objects together) skills to complete a task. With more than one hundred different processes that a welder can utilize, chances are that you will stay busy and interested in your job. There are a wide range of industries to choose from in the welding trades, including everything from car racing to manufacturing.

The median annual salary for welders is $48,940. Plus, you can make additional money through working overtime or earning performance bonuses.

If welding sounds like an interesting career path for you, the first thing you will need to do is earn your high school diploma or GED certificate. Next, you will want to explore the different paths you can take to become a professional welder. You can enter an apprenticeship program, where you work with experienced welders daily, as well as learning more about job safety and the proper use of tools on the job. As you progress, you will be given more complex job tasks such as measuring, cutting, and working with wooden and metal studs. But an apprenticeship isn't the only path into welding. Another option is to enroll in a training program at a trade school or technical college, where you will complete a welding training program and obtain the skills and qualifications that you need to become an entry-level residential or commercial welder. Once you have completed your training and become an entry-level welder, you can begin exploring and advancing your career.

Mason

Laying brick is one of the oldest trades—and one that draws on a variety of skills and abilities. Masonry construction involves using many different building materials such as brick, stone, marble, and granite. As a mason, your job duties include mixing mortar and laying brick, laying floors and stairs, mixing and placing concrete, and creating different wall textures. The average national income of a mason is $53,010 per year. Once you have completed an apprenticeship, you can advance your career by becoming a subcontractor or general contractor.

Painter

If you enjoy the sense of starting fresh and like things being clean and orderly, painting may be the career for you. Painting is an important job. Whenever a new home or commercial building is built, almost all the interior and some of the exterior surfaces need to be painted to protect them from water, mold, and corrosion damage. Painting also helps maintain a home or office's appearance and increases its value. When you choose a career as a painter, you have a variety of responsibilities on the job, including preparing surfaces; mixing colors; applying paint stains, sealers, and finishers; and sanding or water blasting surfaces. The average national wage

Other Interesting Opportunities

There are many career options in the building trades that you are most likely familiar with. But check out some of these unique roles.

Shotcreter. Have you ever been curious about how concrete gets put into walls? The answer is shotcrete. A shotcreter uses a hose to shoot concrete at high speeds into areas including walls, slopes, tunnels, and even swimming pools.

Stonemason. If you like rocks, a career as a stonemason might be right for you. Stonemasons use stones to create architectural structures such as fireplaces, feature walls, and even complete buildings.

Urban designer. Do you think it would be fun to design an urban area, considering factors such as transportation options, land use, and sustainability? Urban designers work closely with architects, engineers, policymakers, and local community members to help bring design ideas to life.

Digital engineering lead. Do you love construction and tech? If so, you may want to consider becoming a digital engineering lead. These professionals utilize tech such as virtual and augmented reality to help improve buildings. They create better plans for buildings by making them more environmentally friendly. Their work helps speed up job projects.

Environmental consultant or manager. Environmental consultants focus on creating and maintaining sustainable construction practices and environmentally friendly designs. They also coach construction teams on how best to use renewable materials, energy-efficient technologies, and eco-friendly practices that help promote sustainability and minimize the impact on the environment.

of a painter is $47,700 per year. Once you have completed an apprenticeship and on-the-job training, there are a variety of jobs to choose from, such as becoming a drywall painter, subcontractor, or residential contractor.

Carpenter

Do you like to build things and see your vision come to life from start to finish? If you choose a career as a carpenter, be prepared to stay busy. Carpenters are needed in many different areas of construction and often work throughout the entire construction process of residential or commercial buildings. That makes it one of the most secure jobs in the building trades industry. In the carpentry trade, you are involved in framing floors, walls, ceilings, and roofs. You also build concrete forms; apply plywood, roof paper, and shingles; build cabinets and countertops; and install doors, windows, trim, and siding. All your hard work pays off; the average national wage of a carpenter is $56,350 per year.

Apprenticeship programs are available to get you started. Helper positions, such as assembling materials and assisting with cutting, shaping, and measuring, will help you get your foot in the door. When you have completed your initial training, you will have your pick of many career opportunities, such as working with home builders, subcontractors, remodelers, and commercial builders.

CHAPTER FIVE

Road to Success

There are many exciting and rewarding job options in the building trades industry. And there are many ways to advance your career and achieve your professional goals. Here are some expert tips and strategies to help you get started on the fast track toward advancing your career in the building trades.

Develop Skills

Constantly learning new things and developing your skills are instrumental in advancing your career in the building trades. Here are some important skills to help you stay competitive in your industry:

Technical Expertise

Work hard to learn and master the technical aspects of your field, including construction techniques, engineering principles, and equipment operations.

Computer literacy is essential in the building trades.

Communication

Improving your communication skills can help you work more effectively with clients, suppliers, and your colleagues.

Problem-Solving

Mastering problem-solving skills will help you overcome work-related challenges and find effective solutions to them.

Project Management

Learning how to improve your project management skills will help you plan, organize, and complete your job more effectively.

There are many other ways to become a skills superstar in the building trades. These include attending workshops and conferences, taking online courses, or completing certifications relevant to your field.

Build a Solid Network

Networking is an effective way to learn about new opportunities in your industry, along with gaining important industry insights. By building and maintaining professional relationships, networking can help advance your career. As the common saying goes, it's not just what you know, but also who you know. Check out the following tips to help build your network.

Attend Industry Events

Make plans to attend trade shows, conferences, and other industry events on a regular basis. This will give you the opportunity to connect with influential professionals and stay up-to-date on industry trends.

Utilize Social Media

Brush up your profile and start meeting and engaging with associates in the building trades through social platforms or join an online industry forum to help expand your virtual network.

Attend building trade shows. Talk to people. Get their information. Even if you don't need that information now, it is helpful to have.

Get Referrals and Recommendations

Don't be afraid to ask for referrals and recommendations from your network; it's a great way to help increase your credibility and visibility in the building trades industry.

Join Professional Associations

Becoming a member of organizations and associations in your industry is a great way to learn more about seminars, training programs, and networking opportunities that you may want to attend. There are associations at the local, state, national, and even international levels.

Build a Strong Résumé

It's important to have experience and skills in your career. However, it's just as important to let people know about them. Remember, your résumé is your professional calling card. Ensure that it is always up-to-date by highlighting accomplishments, certifications, and projects that you have completed, as well as jobs or other roles that you have performed. Don't be afraid to showcase your achievements. This will help hiring managers see why you are the ideal candidate for a promotion or a new position.

Safety First

Practicing safety is of great importance in all career fields, especially in the building trades industry, in which many of the jobs involve using complex tools, machinery, or materials. When you make safety a priority, it shows others that you are a professional and helps make you an asset to your company, team members, and customers and suppliers. Here are some ways that you can emphasize safety in your career:

Continued Training

The building trades industry is continuously changing and evolving. Make sure that you stay up-to-date on safety regulations and practices by participating in training and certification programs.

Leading by Example

Show your company, team members, and customers that you are serious about safety. When you demonstrate a commitment to safety on the job, it will help inspire your associates to do the same, as well as gain the trust of those that work with you each day.

Paying Attention to Detail

There are a lot of things constantly happening on a jobsite. Always be aware of your surroundings, along with what your team members are doing. This will help prevent costly project delays and, most importantly, accidents happening to yourself and others.

Embracing a Can-Do Attitude

Having a positive attitude can help advance your career in the building trades industry. It helps you meet challenges more effectively because you might feel more prepared for them. Plus, when you have a can-do attitude, you will likely gain respect from your team members and managers, which can help expand your network and advance your career. Check out some ways to help build your positive attitude.

Stay Professional

Remember to demonstrate professionalism in all your interactions. This can include being respectful of your team members, clients, and suppliers; performing your job with integrity; and being accountable for your actions.

Stay Resilient

Everyone faces challenges and obstacles. It's important to treat these setbacks as learning opportunities, not failures.

Focus on Continuous Improvement

Be eager to learn ways that you can improve your job skills, knowledge, and performance every day.

Be Solution-Oriented

Try not to beat yourself up or point the finger at others when you face a problem; focus on ways to find solutions rather than dwelling on the issues.

Setting goals is motivating and can improve your focus and job performance and keep you accountable as you move toward a career.

Growth and Demand in the Building Trades

Building trades professionals will be in high demand for the foreseeable future. Older buildings need constant repair. New residential areas mean new houses to build. And as older workers retire, their roles in the workforce will need to be replaced.

These are the careers in the building trades expected to see the fastest growth between 2022 and 2032:

1. Plumbers: 2 percent growth
2. Ironworkers: 2 percent growth
3. Construction workers: 4 percent growth
4. Masons: 3 percent growth
5. Heavy equipment operators: 3 percent growth

If job security, a livable wage, great benefits, and opportunities for advancement sound good to you, the time is right to consider a career in the trades.

Be Flexible

Change is inevitable in all industries, including the building trades. The trades industry is subject to ups and downs in the economy, along with changing demands in the marketplace. Try not to fear change, but to welcome it. Successful building trades professionals realize the importance of being flexible and doing what it takes to stay relevant by embracing change, being open to learning new ways of completing their projects and tasks, and always being willing to tackle different projects to help broaden their experience and skills.

Find a Mentor

Having a mentor in your industry can be a great way to advance your career. An experienced manager, team member, or friend or family member can help provide you with job insights, along with sharing what experiences, training, education, and more have helped them along the way. A mentor can help you face challenges and make informed decisions about your career. They can also offer encouragement and help you stay accountable as you start your journey into adulthood.

Set Clear Career Goals

Plan your work, and then work your plan. Take some time to create a clear, realistic career advancement plan; this will help you stay focused and keep moving in the right direction. Plus, setting attainable goals is a great way to stay motivated as you work toward advancing your career. Create lists of career goals. Do you want to become a faster worker? Is there something

Never be afraid to try something new. The more you know, the better worker you can be.

you'd like to learn? Where do you see yourself in five years? In ten? Figure out which goals are long-term and which are short-term. Will a short-term goal help you attain a longer-term one?

Take Advantage of Leadership Opportunities

One of the best ways to set yourself apart in the building trades industry is by developing and showcasing your leadership skills.

Leadership skills are extremely valuable and can help boost your career prospects. These are some ways to become a leader in your field:

Volunteer for Additional Responsibilities

Be willing to go the extra mile. Ask your manager for the opportunity to take on extra responsibilities or leadership roles on projects that you are working on to help showcase your abilities.

Coach Someone

Offer to train or help a junior professional who is new on the job. This will help demonstrate your leadership qualities and show your supervisors that you want to help contribute to the growth of other team members. They may teach you something new too. Things change. For example, a method you may have learned in your early years could be outdated. A fresh pair of eyes can also help find solutions to problems.

Participate in Continuing Education

Get excited to learn more about ways to advance your career. Completing an industry certification, participating in internal training programs that your employer offers, reading building trades industry publications, attending webinars, and seeking cross-training opportunities are all options to help you learn more about your trade and be a more effective leader.

CONCLUSION

Finishing Touches

The future looks bright for the next generations of workers in the building trades. There are a wide variety of jobs available. With some hard work and a vision, you can choose your own path. Take the first step by exploring what's out there. Learn about what each job does and see if anything in particular sticks out to you. Use some of your newfound tools to meet industry insiders, talk to recruiters and career counselors, and review your own skills to see if there's anything you can do to strengthen your résumé.

There's a job out there for everyone—which means that there's a perfect job for you! Maybe you'll work on the forefront of the latest construction technology. Or you might become an expert painter or welder. Finding the perfect fit will lead to pride in your work and the knowledge that you're making your living doing something you enjoy.

GLOSSARY

apprenticeship: a training program where individuals learn a skill or trade from an experienced person, such as a mentor

career aptitude: tests meant to help people understand the best type of job that suits their interests, skills, and personality

certification: the act of certifying; the state of being certified

commercial: anything involving or related to the buying and selling of goods

contractor: someone who contracts to perform work or provide supplies, such as someone who contracts to construct a building

cross-training: becoming trained to do more than one specific job

fabricated: constructed or manufactured from prepared parts for use in larger products

finishes: attractive surface appearances

general contractor: a person or company responsible for overseeing a construction project

general education development (GED): a set of tests that certify that the test-taker has met high-school level academic skills; also known as a graduate equivalency degree

graduate equivalency: a level of achievement at the same level as finishing a course of study

heating, ventilation, and air-conditioning (HVAC): technology that controls the temperature and quality of the air in an enclosed space

industry: a department or branch of a business, manufacturer, art, or craft

infrastructure: the system of public works of a county, state, or region, or the resources (such as personnel, buildings, or equipment) required for an activity

masonry: stonework

median: being in the middle or in an intermediate position

operating engineer: a person who works with power construction equipment, such as bulldozers, graders, and excavators

referral: a recommendation for a job opening from a current employer or someone in a professional network

remodeler: a person who carries out structural changes to an existing building

residential contractor: an individual or company who contracts directly with an owner to provide work in one or more special skills

resilient: tending to recover from or adjust easily to misfortune or change

résumé: a document that provides a summary of your education, work experience, skills, goals, and accomplishments

salary: a fixed, regular payment, typically paid monthly or bi-weekly, from an employer to an employee

soft skill: any of several personal traits that characterize a person's ability to work with others, including, but not limited to, creativity, time management, leadership, teamwork, and conflict resolution

solder: to join two things with a low-melting metal alloy

subcontractor: a business or person who does work as part of a larger project

weld alignment: a joint between two pieces of metal that have been welded together

SOURCE NOTES

7 “High job satisfaction . . . mentorships and training.”: “Research on Preservation and Restoration Building Trades Reveals Worker Shortages in the Northeast and Highlights Opportunities for Workforce Development,” *New Hampshire Preservation Alliance*, March 28, 2023, https://www.nhpreservation.org/blog/research-study-on-preservation-and-restoration-building-trades.

14 “Graduating from high . . . skills [in school].”: Luke Greiner and Mark Schultz, “Is Graduating from High School Still Relevant?” *Minnesota Department of Employment and Economic Development*, September 2019, https://mn.gov/deed/newscenter/publications/review/september-2019/graduating-highschool.jsp.

25 “If one fully . . . most successful leaders.”: Forbes Coaches Council, “16 of the Best Reasons to Pursue a Professional Apprenticeship,” *Forbes*, September 8, 2021, https://www.forbes.com/sites/forbescoachescouncil/2021/09/08/16-of-the-best-reasons-to-pursue-a-professional-apprenticeship/?sh=767b.

27 “You need a . . . up [working] capacity”: Andrew Dorn, “Labor Crisis: Why Is There a Shortage of Plumbers and Electricians?” *Hill: Changing America*, April 9, 2024, https://thehill.com/changing-america/enrichment/education/4583268-labor-crisis-why-is-there-a-shortage-of-plumbers-and-electricians/.

SELECTED BIBLIOGRAPHY

"Careers in the Construction Trades." National Association of Home Builders. Accessed June 26, 2024. https://www.nahb.org/advocacy/top-priorities/workforce-development/careers-in-the-construction-trades.

"Five Fastest Growing Careers in Construction." Construction Careers Foundation. Accessed June 26, 2024. https://constructioncareers.org/five-fastest-growing-careers-in-construction/.

Genious. "Tips to Advance Your Career in the Construction Industry: A Comprehensive Guide." AllBetter. Accessed June 26, 2024. https://allbetterapp.com/tips-to-advance-your-career-in-the-construction-industry-a-comprehensive-guide/.

Gillis, Jeff. "Top 25 Highest Paying Trade Jobs." Interview Guys, May 24, 2022. https://theinterviewguys.com/highest-paying-trade-jobs/.

Hodges, Sarah. "The Future of Construction Work and Workers." Business and Tech. Accessed June 26, 2024. https://www.futureofbusinessandtech.com/construction-in-america/the-future-of-construction-work-and-workers/.

"Seven Ways for High School Students to Prepare for a Construction Apprenticeship." Construction Careers Foundation. Accessed June 26, 2024. https://constructioncareers.org/seven-ways-for-high-school-students-to-prepare-for-a-construction-apprenticeship/.

"10 Reasons to Choose a Career in the Building Trades." Construct Your Future News, April 25, 2023. https://www.constructyourfuture.com/blog/10-reasons-to-choose-a-career-in-the-building-trades.

FURTHER INFORMATION

Books

Brunson, Paul. *Not Afraid to Work: Practical Advice for the Young Electrician*. Warwick, RI: B.E., 2024.
This guide explains getting an apprenticeship—and then a career—as an electrician.

Klatte, Kathleen A. *Construction Worker*. Buffalo: Rosen, 2025.
Explore the wide variety of opportunities in the construction trade in this informative text.

Mason, P. D. *Skilled Trade Career Planning for Teens: The Handbook of Lucrative Skilled Trades and High Paying Occupations that Don't Require Expensive College Degrees*. Minneapolis: Sugardog, 2023.
Mason provides an in-depth handbook to find a career in the skilled trades, such as reasons to consider a skilled trade, myths about the work, and detailed descriptions of different jobs.

Reeves, Diane Lindsey. *What Construction Managers Need to Know*. Ann Arbor, MI: Cherry Lake, 2024.
Learn from career experts and get a jump start on a career in construction.

Voss, Elizabeth Hobbs. *Become a Construction and Building Instructor*. San Diego: BrightPoint Press, 2024.
Dive into the training and qualifications needed to become a construction and building inspector.

Websites

Best Construction Jobs—Careers

https://money.usnews.com/careers/best-jobs/rankings/best-construction-jobs

US News and World Report ranks the best construction jobs of 2024, including the number of projected job positions, the median salary, and the education needed.

Build Your Future

www.byf.org

This site provides insights into construction careers and learning resources for educators, workers, and industry professionals.

Careers in the Construction Trades

www.nahb.org

The National Association of Home Builders provides resources to help workers connect, learn, and improve their communities.

Construction Career Pathways

constructioncareers.org

Construction Career Pathways challenges members of the trades to realize the dream of building their own future.

Construct Your Future—Careers in the Construction Trades

www.constructyourfuture.com

Learn about the numerous benefits that can be gained through a career in trades.

INDEX

PHOTO ACKNOWLEDGMENTS

Tashi-Delek/E+/Getty Images, p.5; SolStock/E+/Getty Images, p. 10; Red ivory/Shutterstock, p. 12; YinYang/E+/Getty Images, p. 15; Viktor Cvetkovic/E+/Getty Images, p. 17; kali9/E+/Getty Images, p. 18; sturti/E+/Getty Images, p. 21; JonnyGreig/E+/Getty Images, p. 23; monkeybusinessimages/iStock/Getty Images, p. 25; sturti/E+/Getty Images, p. 29; Rawpixel.com/Shutterstock, p. 32; Monkey Business Images/Shutterstock, p. 35; Phynart Studio/E+/Getty Images, p. 39; Jessica Rinaldi/The Boston Globe/Getty Images, p. 45; Xinhua News Agency/Getty Images, p. 47; People Images/iStock/Getty Images, p. 50; People Images.com/Yuri A/Shutterstock, p. 51; sturti/E+/Getty Images, p. 53

Cover image: vitranc/Getty Images